Copyright © 2022 Tekkan
Artwork Copyright © 2022

All rights reserved.
First Printing, 2022
ISBN 978-0-578-38701-7

To contact Tekkan please email:
buddhaboy1289@gmail.com

Table of Contents

Liberty. . . . . Page 1

A *Tyrannosaur* Is a Metaphor . . Page 36

Could a *Tyrannosaur* Allegory . Page 46

River . . . . .Page 74

Cid's Gift . . . . Page 84

How to Read My Poems

I want to be direct in my meaning — I want people to clearly understand my meaning. My wordiness is inspired by Shakespeare, and the (aimed-for) concision is in imitation of Japanese style. Using the sonnet with the *tanka*, I mix the sensibility of the Occident and the Orient — which I have done by living in England, Japan, and America.

I have married the sonnet to the *tanka*. I tell a story in the sonnet. The story builds to a conclusion in the last line. The *tanka* is a commentary, or a counterpoint, to the sonnet — the combined poems have two endings.

I don't punctuate much in my poetry. I want the words themselves to do the work. There is logic between words, and the forms provide structure. By not using punctuation I hope to direct readers to carefully attend to each word — to appreciate the graininess of words.

Reading my poems silently and reading them aloud may be different experiences. There's not always a pause intended at the end of the line.

Hint: *sonnets are to be recited not as lines but as phrases, and a phrase sometimes overflows the break at the end of a line. I pause and take a breath where it seems natural for me to pause. Another person may pause differently than I do.*

Each poem is a piece of a mosaic, and it is my hope that the collection of poems forms a portrait of consciousness.

My daughter, *Jocelyn Figueroa*, is a wonderful artist. Her artwork graces this book.

I am Barry MacDonald. I received the *dharma* name *Tekkan*, which means "Iron Man," a settled practitioner of great determination.

— *Tekkan*

Everyday Mind XXVII

Liberty

Liberty is a challenging ideal
Only a few of us truly grasp it
It takes determination of spirit
And exacting effort to make it real
For most — *our experience is piecemeal* —
It is so much easier to submit
Before we seize it for ourselves we quit
Fulfilling liberty is an ordeal
It's not only about self-reliance
It is more than being merely stubborn
Do you have a *victim mentality*?
Is freedom to be found in defiance?
In *liberation* a new life is born
To flow with the cosmos is to be free.

Can you act without
second-guessing yourself and
without lashes of
fear resentment self-pity?
can you be *spontaneous?*

Snow in early March is very heavy
Rain turned into sleet and snow overnight
Snow-covered branches are a lovely sight
But shoveling wet snow is misery
To do it well one needs to be mighty
This overcast morning is super bright
A high ceiling of clouds is pristine white
It's not a day when I can be lazy
All of the branches of the trees are bare
March is a month when I'm tired of winter
The brown and gray of the trees are so drab
I am looking forward to fresh warm air
If I had my way spring would come sooner
If I'm not mindful I become a crab.

I look forward to
the sweet drifting scent and
the exquisitely
lovely sight of the apple
blossoms beside my driveway.

I'm looking outside and observing drops
Of snowmelt fall from the eaves of the house
And many of the branches have a gloss
Of ice about them — *to the very tops*
Of the trees — and surely the drops will plop
Onto the snow-encumbered ground across
The yards as we are entering the dross
Of winter as the land becomes a slop
Of liquidating snow in afternoon
As yesterday's freezing drizzle is gone
And the blue of the sky is shining bright
And the air will become much warmer soon
But winter isn't done — *it does drag on* —
Could there be last-minute blizzards? There might.

There's no doubt that the
days are getting warmer
now and the sparkle
of the sun is much stronger —
but March is always messy.

During winter months we are inside our
Homes for most of the day which is a drag
And it's no wonder that our spirits *sag*
But in March we have afternoon hours
Of resurgent sun — *even rain showers* —
I may stuff winter in a duffel bag
To encourage myself — *to lollygag* —
A change of attitude lends me powers
There are blue skies inside every season
But a stronger sun is noticeable
The crystals of snow are shining brighter
The long wings of winter darkness are gone
As extending daylight is tangible —
In Minnesota we feel happier.

As winter goes on
we get used to being shut
inside our little
rectangular living rooms
as if there weren't any sky.

Kitcat is a being whom I don't want
To live without and I worry about
His urinary tract and so I doubt
The quality of cat food at Walmart
And I believed that I was being smart
By going to a pet store to seek out
A specialized blend that will winnow out
A blockage — which I think is a small part
For me to play to keep my continued
Companionship with Kitcat — and so I
Paid an expensive price for a hefty
Bag of healthy chewy food which I viewed
As an investment — and it is true I
Want to please myself — *by being guilt-free.*

Kitcat gazed at the
bag sniffed the bits in
the dish looked at me
and wouldn't eat it.

I paid twenty-eight dollars for that bag
When I could have gone to Walmart and spent
Eight and now I see that he won't consent
To eat it which is a pretty price tag
For being a finicky scalawag
So I adopt a determined intent
That I am going to win this argument
And I won't entreat him — *I will not nag* —
Either he eats the food or goes hungry
And he looks at me day after day and
Paws at the bag and he sniffs the food in
The dish and I'm trying not to worry
But he continues not to eat it and
If this is a test of our wills — *he wins*.

To Walmart I go
to get another bag of
rotgut cat food which
to me seems like he's smoking
cigarettes or drinking beer.

Bare branches are swaying in wind today
There are a few wisps of clouds this morning
Maybe the life in the trees is stirring
Does a warming wind play a part? — *it may* —
Do branches stimulate roots when they sway?
In blusters the limbs of trees are flexing
Perhaps the somnolent roots are waking
The tugging on the roots is forceful play
The frozen soil and the slumbering trees
Fit together like a hand in a glove
In the winter the wind is bitter cold
Rigor mortis vanishes by degrees
The tide of the sun is turning above
A warm reviving wind is taking hold.

Along the length of
a barren twig who can say
where the buds of leaves
and flowers will be sprouting?
But *surely* they are coming.

Reading is a sophisticated play
Turning pages — *absorbing ideas* —
Striking ideas on pristine pages
A curious book can be a doorway
A fresh perspective may be a gateway
Sampling words from different ages
Taking lessons from rascals and sages
Seizing the forceful life a book conveys
Poetry appears with my fingertips
The words rise up and they tickle my mind
I'm transported to exotic places
Ingesting phantasy in honeyed sips
Delight with liberation may be twined
I may travel far by turning pages.

The soul of paper
pages holds within itself
the life force of trees
the minerals of the earth
the drops of rain — *and sunshine*.

Each pristine page is a slice of a tree
What you're holding is a substance of earth
Like every living thing it had a birth
Did the tree grow as tall as it could be?
Was it left to flourish as it would be?
I prefer poetry that's down-to-earth
Are these words worthy of the paper's worth?
We are given the gift to simply be
These pages contain the earth's minerals
Seasons of the earth are in this paper
These pages embody the sun and rain
Its color is the same as a snowfall
You are turning pages with your fingers
Feeling proper gratitude is humane.

It's true the living
things of earth go through a
metamorphosis
of forms and experience —
even rocks are transforming.

The open sky without a single cloud
For some reason appears the brightest blue
This is what the atmosphere and sun do
There are some days when the clouds are a shroud
Then there's the drama of the thunderclouds
A prism reveals what the sun can do
All the rainbow colors are shining through
I keep an open mind and I am *wowed*
I love the trees' wild gesticulation
They are standing still and extending out
To the sun every tree is stretching up
Its posture is a kind of devotion
Waiting for bursting growth to come about —
Still until the fire in the sky turns up.

The bare trees in March
symbolize a patience with
an expectancy
of a resurrection in
the form of their budding leaves.

There are ideas about liberty
About opposing the force of Jim Crow
Camps of the Gulag Archipelago
Fighting oppression in society
Wicked abuses of humanity
Taking up arms — lighting a *flambeau* —
And dealing a dictator a death blow
A victory over an enemy
And afterward one nurtures vigilance
Ever watchful wary disputatious
Claiming the virtues of a warrior
Demanding a continued diligence
Countering tyrants and staying jealous
Seeing life as a balance of power.

It is sadly true
there are always clever brutes
through outright power
or through devious lying
who seize control of people.

Disputatious liberty is what we
Have in America which devolves to
Party politics and does so much to
Warp and delude our personalities
Which are embittered in controversies
It's a difficult question — *what to do?* —
Because I don't want to argue with you
And yet I don't see how we can agree
As we are enmeshed in bureaucracy
Leaders of both parties are telling lies
And the effects of lies are *dangerous*
I wish we had quiet sanctuary
Where news wasn't used to antagonize
And elites weren't scheming to deceive us.

The danger isn't
that we won't distinguish the
disrespect and lies
but the real problem is that
we won't recognize the truth.

Liberty in the political sense
Implies the freedom to be left alone
To capture your destiny on your own
And choose a lifestyle of your preference
To be selective in your deference
Worthy education is a touchstone
Where flourishing opinions are well known
Unhindered expression without pretense
Not to be confined by class distinctions
Not to be exploited by the wealthy
Not to be ruled by selfish dictators
Without fear of unjust prosecution
Not to be deprived of prosperity
To escape the trash of monopolies.

To rise from the depth
of poverty through
initiative and
vision is the ideal
of what liberty implies.

We are living in a cynical age
Where news is used to destroy liberty
Events are presented dishonestly
The media headlines inspire rage
The daily narrative promotes outrage
Subtlety is treated cavalierly
What comes through is *victim mentality*
The truth inside events is hard to gauge
The question is — *who is benefiting?* —
Categories of people are exploited
Factions are pitted against each other
Agitation is disorienting
Much too often the innocent are blamed
We get used to fearing one another.

News narratives are
used to create heroes
and villains and truths
that benefit the people
who are controlling the news.

I want readers from different factions
Without the lure of hot-button issues
I'd like my poetry to disabuse
I hope to sidestep hateful reactions
To me agitprop is a distraction
There is no need for personal abuse
From useless debates — *I'd like to get loose* —
I'd rather engender *liberation*
Society is always contentious
The path of liberty is difficult
Maybe people prefer security
It's a virtue to be conscientious
To be open to surprising results
To overcome suffering — *and be free.*

Self-doubt
self-pity
self-criticism
self-disparagement
are devilish.

I'm not a master of philosophy
Who builds cathedrals of ideas
I believe the cosmos is more like jazz
I like poetry that is concept-free
In which it's a joy to go on a spree
Today the sky's the color of topaz
Spring birds are returning with razzmatazz
If you want consistency — *that's not me* —
Underneath the snow the earth is waiting
Rainbow colors are about to explode
The jubilee will start with budding leaves
The breeze in the leaves will soon be sighing
There will be a parade of frogs and toads
I will revert to sandals and short sleeves.

All the winter months
I've seen my bicycle laid
against the wall in
my dining room reminding
me that I am hunkered down.

The quarks are spinning to the left and right
Planets are flowing in gravity swirl
Blood is pulsing in an artery twirl
Heart is beating with a palpable might
All of these facts are escaping my sight
Couch is a creature that lives in a whorl
The oysters in oceans generate pearls
The stars are only visible at night
The horizon is moving very fast
We only see the near side of the moon
You do have a right to be skeptical
I have dreary moods but I let them pass
A handy invention is called a spoon
So much of life is just nonsensical.

I know it's summer
when I close my eyes and *see*
my eyelids are red
and I sense the position
of the *bright* sun by its heat.

I have power to liberate myself
And loathsome people needn't entrap me
I admit that saying so is easy
And it is difficult to calm oneself
How often do you befuddle yourself?
The confabulating mind is busy
How can we stand without getting dizzy?
Do you often try to outsmart yourself?
The magic for me is relaxation
Can I do what I do *wholeheartedly*
Without depending on happy results?
My dilemmas come with expectations
When I want people and things to please me
Too much of my thinking is crazed impulse.

I'd like the ability
to relax no matter what
the circumstances or what
people say.

There are always reasons to despise him
Many people dislike the president
For some his policies are a torment
The raging European war is grim
Chances for an early ending are slim
People justifiably do lament
The news is full of terrible events
Our cup of bitterness reaches the rim
Last year there was another president
People had arguments to hate him too
No matter what happens someone suffers
We take our turns inside predicaments
You don't believe it will happen to you
It seems the economy will get rougher.

One can always
tune into a radio
or a news program
to catch up on the latest
arsenal of ammunition.

I am happy this morning watching snow
I'm ecstatic with this sloppy blizzard
For some I know it's a driving hazard
But by this afternoon this snow will go
It's falling now at a steady tempo
Winter in Minnesota is diehard
With shovels and snow blowers I'm on guard
I'm biding my time like an Eskimo
I'm savoring a taste of nostalgia
I get to bundle in my warmest clothes —
Again — snow is curling from a white sky
This often happens in Minnesota
It's sleety and sloppy and then it goes
I'm grateful for a chance to say *"Goodbye."*

I am seeing flocks
of songbirds flitting between
the bare branches of
trees — birds are frolicking in
the air — *indomitable*.

On this chilly morning my words are birds
The branches are reaching into the sky
The leaves will be coming to dandify
I'm looking about and playing with words
My lines are bouncing and being absurd
These sunny days the birds will multiply
The leaves in the breezes are lullabies
It isn't spring yet but we're on the verge
The birds aren't idle and are not lazy
They possess these trees and want to be here
They come from the south and fly all the way
They flock and they flicker between the trees
With lighthearted songs for a sonneteer
The air will be full of their roundelays.

It's too chilly to
open my windows yet but
soon I will step
outside and be surprised by
boisterous birdsong again.

It's good to focus on simple pleasures
To notice the rhythm in lines of words
And not to care if the meaning's absurd
To pontificate and say — *horsefeathers* —
To count syllables in easy measures
To ignore the news and glorify birds
Who wants to be trapped inside of a dirge?
Is it likely that a horse has feathers?
From a mirror's view — *aren't people crazy?*
Can you find solace in catechisms?
What dictators do is deplorable
It's not so bad to read and be lazy
I sling words to escape cynicism
A foolish poem is adorable.

Use the nimble tips
of your fingers to turn this
page and cast your eyes
upon absurdly written words
of *phantasmagoria*.

I think I'm due for an *epiphany*
I haven't had a surprise for a while
A turning of events that makes me smile
I've noticed that I've gotten fidgety
Which seems to happen when I'm finicky
The same old happenings do not beguile
To be repetitive isn't my style
My thoughts shouldn't assume a fixity
I spend my days looking out a window
I sit in a chair distilling my thoughts
Every day I watch the seasons go by
I net the clouds inside of my lingo
I deplore the trap of being *ersatz*
The world's slippery — *I need to be sly*.

For the first time
in months the sun
is lighting up
my closed eyelids
the brightest red.

Yesterday was fetchingly crisp to walk
Outside so I left my stationary
Bike spontaneously and happily
Early enough to disregard the clock
Liberating myself by taking stock
Of water running precipitously
Across the streets following gravity
Flowing to the river by city blocks
And I was measuring the distance with
Lackadaisical strides watching melting
Snow savoring the resurgent fresh air
Ambling over the bridge noting the pith
Of the afternoon sun resurrecting
Life — and I even saw a woolly bear.

I followed my summer
road bicycle route with
an eye out for trouble
and saw the stubborn ice
in shadowy places.

What do white roses have to do with me?
In late spring they bloom on my patio
About the time the grass begins to grow
After the blossoms of the apple trees
Roses synchronize with the peonies
Roses and peonies are simpatico
Together they make a lovely combo
What do peonies have to do with me?
Lilacs bloom along with apple blossoms
One has to be close to notice their scent
Their scent is fragrant to entice the bees
Bees also bumble with cherry blossoms
Not one of these flowers costs me a cent
They all come along with breeze in the leaves.

All of these flowers —
except for cherry blossoms —
bloom beside my home
which gives me something to look
for — *seasonal companions.*

Not everything I think is important —
I know that may be a surprise to you —
My thoughts tend to organize in a queue
Some notions seem to be inadvertent
While others happen to be discordant
I may see something which becomes a cue
Or else I'm *gobsmacked* looking for a clue
My thoughts are not a Gregorian Chant —
I have noticed that Kitcat has tassels
Of hair bursting inside of his ears and
I wonder if there's a sensual
Significance that perhaps resembles
Whiskers — my ears cultivate hair too and
I don't know why — *it is questionable*.

I've often wondered
whether a *Tyrannosaur*
possessed whiskers and
if so would the whiskers
supplement supremacy?

A sonnet is just a pattern of words
Maybe it's worthy — *maybe it's crazy—*
To write more than one — *one can't be lazy —*
Nonsensical sonnets would be absurd
It's not sacrilege to write about birds
I've tried very hard and have been busy
Writing sonnets doesn't make me dizzy
I will not say that my sonnets are turds
Each sonnet serves as an incantation
There's an air of formality with rhymes
Which lends the words a sense of *importance*
Sonnets don't earn much remuneration
I'm able to make people smile sometimes
And I even made a person laugh — *once.*

I fish in the air
for suitable words and on
occasion the words
and syllables fall into
place — *does that make poetry?*

It is a gift that we give each other
It'd be a shame to take it for granted
When I'm able to it feels enchanted
To simply converse with one another
As if we were all sisters and brothers
Easeful humorous sincere and candid
It is a thrill to be comprehended
Last night we aimed to be happy — *we were* —
Today we wish to be open — *we are* —
There needs to be compatibility
It is the most natural of pastimes
Doing it often builds a repertoire
To be genuine takes some honesty
I suffer when I lack it — *oftentimes*.

If you are reading
this poem you probably
have read many of
my words and so across time
and space we've become friends.

Is our meeting merely accidental?
Do we not influence one another?
Even when we barely know each other?
Is the briefest commerce incidental?
Can it only be coincidental?
What kind of universe do you prefer?
What type of subtleties do you infer?
Do questions make you temperamental?
There is a vast variability
I would like the ability to grow
To be sensitive to slight gradations
Especially with instability
When I'm under pressure can I let go
Of stubborn closed-minded dispositions?

We touch each other
with absence
indifference
insouciance
and defiance.

There's more than we dream of above our heads
We have arrived at the spring equinox
Which is appointed within nature's clock
Another resurrection lies ahead
There is a vast emptiness overhead
And beneath our feet there is molten rock
At times the cosmos is a tinderbox
The magma's burning beneath the seabed
The fire in the sky is gathering strength
Warmth is penetrating the atmosphere
Latent growth is on the point of bursting
The hours of daylight are gaining in length
The earth is a gestating biosphere
The rivers will soon be overflowing.

Galaxies orbit
interminably
and explode
intermittently.

My daughter is a fabulous artist
Her sewn foxes are in a gallery
Her paintings display subtle majesty
Her designs and talent are on target
The trick will be to pinpoint a market
How does one become a celebrity?
By promoting oneself aggressively?
She's at the whims of a fickle market
She sewed a dainty white fox with red eyes
The fox is sitting with its front legs crossed
On the wall behind something is festooned
There's a painting on the wall — it's disguised
On white paint a white primer is embossed
Looking *alertly* you can spot the moon.

Jocelyn Figueroa
painted a glowing full moon
in the subtlest of light
behind a fox with red eyes —
you may not even see it.

We have to take our humor as it comes
Who wants to be with a biting sourpuss?
Disenchanted distracted — in a fuss?
Like the discordance of a crazy drum
A pounding jackhammer in the eardrums?
Assume that nothing is superfluous
Even in the instance it may concuss
Or be nagging trouble — *like bleeding gums* —
Take for instance *Tyrannosaurus rex*
A fearsome biped that's always eating
You'd like to avoid it if possible
The emotions it summons are complex
When spotted it's best to be retreating
We tend to think it is unstoppable.

I like to imagine
The mighty *T. rex* in
a kerfuffle because it
it pinched a puny
forelimb — *so it's whimpering.*

People tend to think we are important
That the earth couldn't get on without us
We are always in a terrible fuss
And masses of people are discordant
Some personalities are abhorrent
I'm trying not to be a sourpuss
It's much worthier to be nonplussed
Our daily narratives make us mordant
We are subject to the equinoxes
Subordinate to the solstices
We are taking a ride on the cosmos
We construct for ourselves little boxes
Ignoring the tugs of the vortices
And we don't have to be so lachrymose.

We didn't give ourselves
the gift of consciousness
and consciousness may not
be quite so easily
dispensed with after death.

My thoughts are not a Gregorian Chant
I'm watching my internal monologue
I notice that I am a demagogue
How often do I tell myself "*I can't*"?
So is it any wonder that "*I won't*"?
Getting through my own thinking is a slog
The veiling of my thoughts is like a smog
I disparage myself within a rant
But I practice the art of letting go
My thoughts do not determine who I am
I know emotions are temporary
From one to another emotions flow
Can I release the negative? — *I can* —
When the smog lifts there is a clarity.

I can't suppress one
angry thought with another
more passionate thought
but I can lovingly let
disharmony *dissipate*.

Each of us is a stream of consciousness
Thought follows thought follows thought follows thought
Emptiness in between is a blind spot
I confabulate so much with my distress
Relaxation is the key to finesse
Thought alone creates perplexing knots
I've gotten more entangled when I've fought
I am much happier when I quiesce
The warmth of a jacket is delicious
The electric hum of a printer is slight
The flowing of the breath is seductive
Rain from a gray sky is mysterious
Sun filtered through the clouds is daylight
The vastness of quiet is attractive.

I can't solve problems
with the force of thoughts alone —
encouragement from
quiet vastness supplements
my river of consciousness.

A *Tyrannosaur* Is a Metaphor

A *Tyrannosaur* is a metaphor
It is a toothy and blundering brute
It's worse than a lizard in a lounge suit
A smelly stupid executioner
You'd rather not meet a *Tyrannosaur*
It's a pandemonium absolute
Its chomping and swallowing isn't cute
It's a terrible primogenitor
It may be a symbol for bad *karma*
A simile for a bloody ending
Paying the consequences from before
But you may counter *karma* with *dharma*
Watching your thoughts may be enlightening
You'd better not meet the Tyrannosaur.

You'd rather not be
a twinkle in a
Tyrannosaur's eye
as nothing good can
come from that.

It can't decide whether it's rain or snow
Are these grains of snow or drops of water?
The sky was gray but it's getting whiter
There is no such thing as the *status quo*
All of nature is a vanishing flow
Spring isn't here — *it is coming later* —
Winter is lasting a few days longer
Do you know? Where did the equinox go?
But once on the ground the grains become drops
And the drops dissipate into the earth
The air is moist and birds are frolicking
The earth isn't frozen — *it is a sop* —
The earth's preparing another rebirth
I don't care what it looks like — *this is spring*.

The grains have become
big watery flakes of snow
blowing sideways in
the wind — *the air's not icy* —
it's merely moist and chilly.

These syllables have a frolicsome beat
Iambic pentameter is boring
Under its influence I'd be snoring
I do prefer predictable heartbeats
But rigid meter is like wearing cleats
It's better to be playfully skipping
Freer than Elizabethan lisping
Perhaps it is true that I like to cheat
It's my game and I'm playing by my rules
It's my aim to entertain you and me
Each poem is a little different
Polysyllabic words are nifty tools
Spoiling expectations makes me happy
I don't want you to be indifferent.

In my world
phantasmagoria
rules and
Tyrannosaurus rex
exist.

It's hectic preparing to take a flight
I will have to get up at 3 a.m.
Finish breakfast by 4 a.m. — then *scram*
I don't want the schedule to be too tight
Forgetting my I.D. would be a fright
Drive and park and *skedaddle* on a tram
The crowd through security's often jammed
The details on my ticket must be right
I will be flying to Dallas Texas
At a window seat for watching the clouds
Summoning to mind the Greek God Hermes
Air travel is a curious nexus
Crammed in a seat while the engines are loud
Aerial — while scrunching up with cramped knees.

All the way to the
check-in baggage counter I'm
pulling on a cord
connected to my wheeled
suitcase containing my stuff.

I will be encountering the gab of
The Philadelphia Society
A coterie of prim sobriety
Which I suppose I'll be a member of
Though the conversation may be above
Me as they possess notoriety
While I'm a weevil in the granary
A ragamuffin who is thinking of
How to confabulate myself with these
Lawyers academics and journalists
Who've been associated for decades
Who are comfortable with their expertise
Even as my self-consciousness persists —
I don't give a damn about accolades.

The most painful
hurdle is the
cocktail hour when
we stand exposed
within circles.

People who think they are important have
Egos that will emanate waves of shock
Upon their peers who are forced to take stock
Of themselves and the waves will surely halve
The unprepared schmuck who can only salve
Distress by fleeing but the waves are schlock
And the aggrandizing egos are crocks —
Though such shocking waves will function like valves
For powerful people — I have found that
Within the coteries of connected
Politicos there are those who look for
Earnestness and authenticity that
Is a smaller coterie selected
To do some good — *which is a worthy core.*

I do my best not
to be intimidated by
aggressive chutzpah
while surfing the disturbing
waves and looking for friendlies.

I took a walk before the conference
Looking for the grassy knoll of Dealy
Plaza because in 1963
President Kennedy — *who was a prince* —
Was assassinated right there and since
That day there is undying mystery
Cloaking an American tragedy
Resonating from a mere six seconds —
I spotted the sixth-floor window of the
School Book Depository building on
Elm Street where the open-air limousine
Was and I viewed the "X" symbols on the
Asphalt where the President was struck on
His neck and head — *this was the bloody scene.*

The images from
the Zapruder film are seared
in the memories
of every American
who experienced those days.

Let these words resemble migrating birds
It's the flocks that reliably appear
Returning in spring and bringing their cheer
Let the mind absorb these transient words
Playful and buoyant like jubilant birds
Like the indigo buntings and killdeer
Like robins and swallows they reappear
Let these words be a net to catch bluebirds —
Remember — this is a vanishing world
The pattern outlasts each living being
Each singular heartbeat will disappear
While the galaxies continue to whirl
Year after year the birds will be singing
It's fragility that makes life so dear.

Individuals
inevitably vanish
while the patterns of
things gradually shift —
even rocks disintegrate.

Tommy Thomson and I pilfered sugar
Cubes from a drawer in the basement of the
Prim Congregational church without a
Qualm while my father was the minister
Which in truth made the deed much funnier
As we hungered for excitement in the
Small boring town of Bayport upon the
Sunday mornings which we made happier
By being clever as we had to be
There and generally didn't enjoy
The serious moralizing project
Invoking our *responsibility*
Which isn't easy for nine-year-old boys
Which we impishly resolved to reject.

The basement of the
Congregational church
in Bayport Minnesota
was the site of our
sweet rebellion.

I drive past the parsonage where we lived
On occasion and the house has a new
Section — built with a second story too —
And although our residence was short-lived
The home inspires memories composed
Of echoing visions of what ensued
On our arrival from Kansas imbued
With titillating shock and dumbfounded
Joy — *Bayport wasn't flat but sported hills* —
An irresistible provocation
For the clunky bicycles that we rode
As we hungered for undeluded thrills
In headlong downhill acceleration
Imitating Evel Knievel mode.

The same willow and
the little creek are beside
the house and I drive
down the identical slope —
but where has the thrill gone?

Could a *Tyrannosaur* Allegory

Could a *Tyrannosaur* allegory
Inspired by a *Tyrannosaur's* bite
Descending from a *Tyrannosaur's* height
Be interpreted as a comedy
Or a societal commentary
Picturing an unpredictable plight
Encountering unopposable might
As unexplainable calamity?
Bald-pated Tyrannosaur — you are done —
You were an odious oppressive beast
You were fearsome once but you can't catch me
You were majestic — but now you are gone —
I will not be your Cretaceous feast
So whatever you do you can't eat me.

If it lived today
Perhaps we could bell
the *Tyrannosaur*
and we would hear it
from around buildings.

An alligator allegory could
Be acceptable as we do have the
Example of *Animal Farm* where the
Pigs became the righteous heroes but would
A *Tyrannosaur* be fitting and would
That animal be suitable when the
Earth was devoid of humans during the
Cretaceous period so therefore should
This poet pick a more appropriate
Protagonist for his allegory?
I will argue that the *Tyrannosaur*
Is a worthy choice to expropriate
From human hearts — *it's not illusory* —
Nothing is worse than a Tyrannosaur.

I don't know about you
but I suspect there are
Tyrannosaurs lurking
behind every building.

I'd love to direct the *Tyrannosaur*
I could even employ a musician
While having it eat a politician
You could call me the *Tyrannosaur Czar*
I hope you don't think that this is bizarre
I could arrange the juxtaposition
To better promote a celebration
Of a violin and *Tyrannosaur*
For the ceremony I'd be untouched
Even though I'd be the instigator
I'd rise above responsibility
I suppose the audience would be hushed
While expecting the executioner
With violinist virtuosity.

A *Tyrannosaur*
nowadays is nothing more
than a metaphor
for unrecognized anger
and simmering resentment.

My Mom doesn't appear at the window
She doesn't notice me when I arrive
She can't really hear me when I drive
There's frailty now — *she's gotten slow* —
The effort of moving cramps her tempo
And yet a persisting patience survives
A curious empathy even thrives
Occasional stubbornness plainly shows
The grand piano's in the living room
The old oak rocking chair remains in place
All of the houseplants continue to grow
The drawers and closets are filled with heirlooms
It's not easy to find an empty space
She is comfortable with mementos.

The kitchen table
the dining room table
are where they always were
but my Mom doesn't cook much
anymore.

Lifting weights is poetry in motion
And the living room is my citadel
That hosts a one-hundred-pound dumbbell
Which I handle with utmost devotion
With enthusiastic locomotion
My lifting resembles a villanelle
Or perhaps an acrobatic rondel
I cast a spell with an iron potion
I also spin my stationary bike
Going for miles without leaving the room
Its operation is a rhapsody
Its steel machinery is music-like
Entertaining me in the afternoon
My breath and heart are beats in harmony.

Through the winter months —
without having to please a
wife — I have used my
living room as a gym and
Kitcat isn't complaining.

When lying awake before the dawn my
Image appears in a funhouse mirror
All my good intentions have gone awry
And I dwell with annoyance and terror
I am aware my view is distorted
That I'm not seeing myself as I am
That my personality's contorted
I do blame myself and may also damn
The others who are entangled with me
My mind's consumed with justification
I'd like to be asleep but I'm not free
From regrets and consequent reactions
I cannot sleep and I can't stop thinking
I might as well be up and get moving.

I get busy with
brushing and feeding Kitcat
and breakfast and then
a busy optimism
dissolves the funhouse mirror.

It's a good question — *what is sanity?* —
I believe that we each have tricky moods
Smoothed over with civilized courtesy
Papering-over restive attitudes
Society can be a tinderbox
Our edgy comedians tweak our nerves
Each politician — *a jack-in-the-box* —
Do we get the leaders that we deserve?
I propose that it's true together we
Dwell inside a hall of funhouse mirrors
On law and liberty we don't agree
Juggling to discourage war and terror
How *precisely* do we see each other?
Do we each reflect distorted mirrors?

The fool who doubts himself
may have more sanity
than a politician
who is certain.

The moon is veiled by the luminous clouds
The browns and grays are still predominant
The gloom of impending showers enshrouds
And the earth appears to be somnolent
Turkey vultures are soaring in circles
Flocks of songbirds flitter between the trees
The vultures reveal the unseen thermals
The bare branches are swaying in the breeze
One learns to appreciate glowing light
That the light penetrates veils upon veils
What a gift it is that we possess sight
Through the vastness of night the light prevails
I can wait to see the afternoon moon
Colors of the rainbow are coming soon.

The resplendent moon
that floats in the after noon
in an empty sky
luminously pacifies
passions as it mystifies.

I don't have to try too hard to be free
But the trick is mindless relaxation
Without expecting to be trouble-free
Without avoiding life's sharp serration
One doesn't learn without the suffering
Touching dead ends inside a labyrinth
Choosing between evils is dumbfounding
We put unworthy statues on our plinths
My problem is that I am striving *hard*
I need more patience to allow what comes
I'd like to be graceful in handling *shards*
To balance patience and action in sums
I am compulsive to make things happen
And the same old patterns happen again.

The cosmos is happening
the Big Bang continuing
lawfully manifesting —
*I am making my choices
and surfing the responses.*

Every year I watch until it happens
I anxiously wait till the snow is gone
I am aware it so often depends
On April vagaries that drag along
Such gloomy days but with experience
I know the last residue of winter
Without the slightest doubt of variance
Will be along the street as it occurs
That snowplows leave behind the highest piles
So the remnant of icy snow will be
Somewhere along the road — *which is a trial* —
Because it doesn't melt — *which bothers me* —
A stubborn bit of winter won't let go
While I am waiting for the grass to grow.

I don't care about
the higher piles around
the parking lots in
town — *winter ends for me*
when my yard is free of snow.

I know I'm being silly — *I don't care* —
That the cosmos is larger than my yard
And it's not important what happens here
Mine isn't a Parisian boulevard
Africa has its hippopotami
The giraffes never think about the snow
The Milky Way exists beyond our sky
There are beautiful tropical grottoes
I don't have a view of Rocky Mountains
Nothing compares with Jupiter's red spot
I'm behaving like a tragedian
My yard is only a minuscule dot
But the last bit of snow is important
Its stubborn persistence is discordant.

A Minnesota
winter in March and April
resembles a trudge
within a tundra and the
horizon remains gloomy.

There is an ash tree in Pioneer Park
On the bluff that overlooks the river
The difference from other trees is stark
The lower limbs were trimmed — *it's grown taller* —
It's impressively wide and also straight
Then it has these weirdly curling branches
The straight trunk and branches don't correlate
How did it come to the shape that it is
With this *frantic pattern* of flyaway
Twigs? I have thought that it's an oddity
Sprouting a disharmonious array
Of parts composing a monstrosity
But the ash is perfectly natural
It's fiercely strong and asymmetrical.

In summer its leaves
supersede any
idea of its
disharmony and
each leaf tastes the sun.

I have my ideas of symmetry
In every line I'm counting syllables
I'm putting effort into constancy
Being regular is respectable
But nature isn't so fastidious
It exults in phantasmagoria
Generating a hippopotamus
A tyrannosaur bespeaks its chutzpah
Over time a river carves a canyon
Spontaneously a volcano erupts
An asteroid will hit the earth again
Each spinning quark is in a constant flux
I suppose that by counting syllables
Wackadoodle becomes *digestible*.

We think a peacock
is beautiful and
it is but also
quite an oddity.

The sky this morning is resplendent blue
Its vibrations are optimistic jazz
We've been patient and spring is overdue
Nature has been veiling its razzmatazz
My hulking cottonwood is standing bare
With its grooves of bark and twisting branches
There's not a hint of buds within the air
It's frozen in time inside quiescence
But I can see cottonwood leaves turning
They flicker and sparkle in summer breeze
I imagine the leaves are bells pealing
A thousand melodious tinkles please
Up and down the cottonwood's lofty height
The turning leaves are rhapsody in light.

An empty sky and
a crescent moon *conceal*
the cosmos beyond —
the chilly air this morning
stimulates reveries.

The margin on the left is a straight edge
There isn't a smidgen of variance
It serves the poem as a solid wedge
Anchoring poetry with common sense
Each line is alive with frolicsome words
They resonate with nonsensical beats
Without an edge the words would be absurd
It launches and restrains my happy feet
Each line is skipping as far as it can
Joyously dancing with ten syllables
The width of each line extends its wingspan
Reciting some words may be a mouthful
The margin on the right has ragged ends
Around the quirky rhymes the poem bends.

Sometimes when writing
poetry I pretend that
I am a mason
using words instead of stones
making airy monuments.

What does the air do to a butterfly?
Do the breezes spur metamorphosis?
How much depends upon the sifting sky?
It's a balance within impermanence
The moon in the sky is a common sight
It's been a beacon to every human
In the afternoon it is not so bright
It has the subtleties of a woman
The sun has always been predominant
Even over white skies with curling snow
The sun burns while the earth is somnolent
The sun is a persistent dynamo
Roses are details of sweetest delight
They are dependent on the bursting light.

The earth persists as
a little blue dot within
a universal
nothingness that is somehow
provocatively pregnant.

Doing anything takes organizing
A complex task demands careful choices
There is the trick of prioritizing
It takes practice to make good decisions
There's satisfaction within excellence
But excellence depends on subtlety
One needs perception to have elegance
It's vital to come with humility
Because excellence is elemental
It roots reside within seeming chaos
It's propitiously accidental
Everything human connects with pathos
It takes humbling discipline to let go
And minimize aggrandizing ego.

Isaac Newton
revealed rainbows
of sunlight
by refining
glassy prisms.

I remember sitting on a limestone
Bluff when I was twelve or thirteen years old
With an acquired taste for being alone
Within a sacred moment — *feeling bold* —
I probed existence with curiosity
I wanted to grasp the meaning of time
With adolescent grandiosity
Seeing downtown Stillwater was sublime
Battle Hollow was there beneath my feet
Where the Sioux defeated the Iroquois
My knowledge of details was incomplete
Imagining the combat was a joy
I wanted to discover what time is
And how it's different from what it was.

I pictured vanished
paddlewheel steamboats
chimneyed lumber mills
mansions of lumber barons
the bars and the bordellos.

There is innocence in adolescence
I was scared of approaching puberty
The challenges of High School were immense
Couldn't admit my insecurity
Being undersized I fought with my fists
Through each lesson I waited for trouble
There were excited mobs to watch my fights
These were bruising imbecilic squabbles
I struggled with reading and writing words
Compared with others I painfully was
Solitary and socially backward
These were disoriented years because
I doubted whether I was good enough
So what I did was ostentatious bluff.

I hadn't experienced
the point of *frustration*
and *exhaustion* after
which comes
relaxation.

I've been pulling a gag on my readers
You have put too much of your faith in me
I must admit that I am a cheater
I can't even describe a simple tree
Things of the world are beyond *depiction*
Only when you see it does it look real
And tasting truly *beggars* description
Beethoven's symphonies are ideal
Afterward there is only memory
Is a photograph worth a thousand words?
Even a picture is illusory
To pretend it's dynamic is absurd
The ancient Chinese painters had a point
A few ethereal lines don't disappoint.

A
tongue
and
banana
become
one.

Billions of men parade furry faces
But not every beard appears attractive
I grow hair in unusual places
The insides of my ears are productive
My upper lip has a caterpillar
White hair is blossoming upon my chin
I don't see all my hairs in a mirror
So why bother with the hairs on my shins?
It's fashionable now to grow stubble
I'm growing a beard to see if it's white
There will be a week of itchy trouble
Until it thickens I'm an awful sight
Hairs on faces are like branches of trees
Some patterns are a weird cacophony.

Checking in a
mirror doesn't
make a beard grow
any faster.

It is fifty degrees this afternoon
I won't get on my stationary bike
My road bicycle is repaired and tuned
I'm savoring an adrenalin spike
With racing pants and a long-sleeved jersey
I'm going to sleekly cut the air today
Pedaling inside would be unworthy
It was respectable just yesterday
Standing in my short pants my legs look pale
After winter I'm pathetically pink
It is the same as if I'd been in jail
My bicycle sounds a musical clink
The tires are revolving upon the rug
The air outside is an exciting drug.

I'm going to be
like a bird today
pedaling as though
my legs were wings
stressing lungs and heart.

Afternoon warmth only lasts a few hours
Mornings and evenings remain quite chilly
There's always a chance for April showers
I am seizing my opportunity
Stillwater's streets are refreshingly steep
I descend inside a full-body plunge
Turning around corners in graceful sweeps
Absorbing new sensations like a sponge
Out of town there's a slope extending up
I rise from the seat as if I'm running
And the strain on my breath is building up
Every passing landmark I'm recalling
I will need to regain the strength I had
And losing some weight wouldn't be so bad.

From three to five
p.m. sights breezing
seem an oasis
apart from the
clinging cold.

The wind's pushing me on the Crossing Bridge
Which towers above the St. Croix River
It's about as long as the Brooklyn Bridge
With the wind helping me — *I go faster* —
I've taken this route many times before
Every passing landmark is like a cue
I am remembering what to look for
Just after the bridge I know what to do
Up off the seat I will charge up the hill
I measure myself against memory
My ability is less than my will
I'm out of shape — *I am not laggardly* —
Pedaling on a stationary bike
Is not at all like a *genuine bike.*

I'm a bird with
wheels instead of
wings — the rippling
river reflects
sky dappled clouds.

The steel machinery served its purpose
I exercised inside my living room
I avoided becoming a sourpuss
Throughout the length of winter's icy gloom
The stationary bike kept me busy
My legs revolved at a furious pace
At the end of an hour I was sweaty
The ceiling and walls were a happy space
There weren't any slopes to challenge my breath
I didn't shift gears to meld with the land
The fickle wind never tested my strength
Without opportunity of a tan
There weren't the natural spurts and rests
I wasn't able to summon my best.

The aluminum
frame of the bike is like
the spare skeleton
of a bird enabling
lofty flight.

Meditation and coffee afterward
Is a recipe for baking poems
I leisurely linger and summon words
RhymeZone.com is a potent potion
It is fun to measure with syllables
It's a joy to deploy both "p"s and "b"s
I can even make sense — *if I'm able* —
In coming days I will write about bees
I am having an ordinary life
Which can't be described in Hollywood style
I am doing my best to avoid strife
It would make me happy to have you smile
I wait for words — *and they suddenly come* —
Concocting nonsense with the rising sun.

With a quiet mind
it's not hard to make something
of a lengthy slope
of the bare branches swaying
or of a vanishing bird.

How much better it is to be one of
A companionship without needing to
Be the celebrity cynosure of
Such a fellowship where one can come to
Communicate and to comprehend each
Other without needing to establish
An impeccable prominence to reach
Parity without being standoffish
Without having to be someone other
Than who one genuinely is — so that
We may discourse as brothers and sisters
Which is so starkly different from what
Other clubby coteries ask of us
As anyone can join us — *without fuss*.

Alcoholics and
addicts who want to be
sober together
have already paid dearly
to share our companionship.

One of us that day was *Japanese* and
Others were *British* and *Canadian* —
But on this day there was a German — and
There were the usual *Americans*
And one *Australian* composing a clique
And confab of six nationalities
In a sum of seven alcoholics
And we weren't in a bar taking our ease
But we were a fellowship of those who
Would rather not be drinking today so
We came to a small room in a church to
Talk on Tuesday afternoon in *Kyoto
Japan* and our gab was ordinary —
Our mission was extraordinary.

I feel sorry for
normal people who don't have
such bright memories —
this one resonating from
some 30 years ago.

River

Multiple sclerosis takes a toll on
Her during the long-frozen winter months
But she is even more afflicted on
Those days of the clammy and chilly months
Of March and April and when she leaves home
She takes along the numbing medicine
To minimize spasms that often come
Which shoot through like electrical zaps in
Her legs and so she wears layers of clothes
When meeting friends with typical courage
Because there is no evading — *she knows* —
Of the outlook of living on the edge
Of discomfort which she does cheerfully
Taking all prudent precautions daily.

She is not one to
passively abide in her
wheelchair — she knows where
she's going and she has a
knack for being dramatic.

I think of the sonnet form as a mold
Into which I pour verbiage as if
Words were infinitely malleable
And definitions were only mischief
Thusly I may not be predictably
Logical because when I start a line
I'm trying to make a rhyme cleverly
And I may not make much sense every time
That you come to the end of a line so
Be aware that my sonnets are a trick
Of enticing my readers' eyes to flow
Pell-mell to the end where there is a kick
Of a rhyming couplet which I do hope
Won't leave you convinced that I am a dope.

*Just think of my words
as the clowns inside of a
clown car with all the
miscreants running amok
once they are liberated.*

I've found it's true — *something comes from nothing* —
The window stimulates my empty head
There's discovery in playful wording
To put a finger on what's left unsaid
Within a poem I don't have a goal
I juggle notions to see what happens
I like to think that my mind is a bowl
Each of us possesses a cosmic lens
How does it come that words have leverage?
I keep my eyes on nonsensical truth
To get tangled in thoughts is average
It's adventure that entices a sleuth
A poem is nothing more than wordy breath
Reverberating with questions is best.

There is a taste of truth called
verisimilitude
beyond sensual proof.

Can you picture a tyrannosaur smile?
What would it look like if it were happy?
Would it be capable of subtle guile?
A quantity of curiosity?
Do you think — *like a dog* — it wagged its tail?
Was it ever fretful and lachrymose?
In some ways was the tyrannosaur frail
With disabilities to diagnose?
Can you imagine that it lives in you
Sublimating the tyrannosaur bite
Coming from the primordial stew
Manifesting in an urge to smite
Transmogrifying with *esprit de corps*
The politics of a tyrannosaur?

The tyrannosaur
is a metaphor
for primordial
incorporeal
appetite.

At my window we've arrived at the time
Of the season by midmorning when the
Sun becomes propitious for seedtime
As light is surprisingly bright with a
Coaxing insistence that what was asleep
Buried in the soil should burst open and
Sprout as a medley of rain and sleet seeped
Into the earth which is receptive and
Soft and I can no longer sit at my
Desk without wearing a brimmed hat that shades
My sight from the blaze which tickles my wry
Play of humor as spring has been delayed
For many weeks but apparently not
Forever — soon it may even be hot.

The air is damp and
chilly while light radiates
through the glass turning
my closed eyelids brilliant red
and I know where the sun is.

Among my friends and even within me
I'm wary of arousing a latent
Tyrannosaur because we disagree
And I don't make my opinions blatant
Because public discourse is divided
Over surface-level identity
And certain topics are best avoided
When propaganda uses history
To categorize and to stigmatize
And I yearn to be able to express
How our politicos have weaponized
Our cultural language which makes a mess
For well-intended communication
Which desires reconciliation.

More important than
opinion is
forgiveness
relaxation
and gratitude.

The black letters on the page embody
The intelligence of culture in their
Organized shapes upon which we agree
Which vowels and consonants that we will pair
With which letters together consisting
Of syllables and words that codify with
Rigidity what the words mean losing
The artistry of ancient hieroglyphs
Perhaps but melding our mechanical
Sophistication to our up-to-date
Logical sensibility with all
Our perspicacity — *which may be great* —
And our letters are worthy metaphors
For slowly accumulated splendor.

We can almost fool
ourselves — yet beneath it all
under layers of
sophisticated piffle
we remain *whackadoodle*.

The black letters on white pages also
Point to a way of misunderstanding
Because we aren't good at seeing the whole
Picture but get fixated absorbing
Only a half of it as it's easy
To follow the words flowing on the page
And I am certainly a devotee
Of the words but we overlook the stage
On which the letters play as it's the white
Paper pages that makes words visible
And without empty pages we'd lose sight
Of letters — so it's inconceivable
To have the black letters that mean something
Without white pages that stand for nothing.

Galaxies and space
fish and water
birds and sky
mind and void
are what is.

It's average to be busy with thoughts
Our eyes will be seeing — *our minds thinking* —
It's only human to ignore blind spots
Politics is about leveraging
Emotions that connect with narratives —
People give their hearts to painful stories
We get tangled within injustices
We judge each other with categories —
A nation is governed with ruthless guile
Manipulating gullibility
And masses of people are volatile
Power is seized through negativity
Our news is throbbing with accusation
We are overburdened with frustration.

Fashions of
the ruling class
morph but there
are always
injustices
and scapegoats.

I formulate opinion as I go
Depending on principles that I trust
There are daily arguments to follow
I have my share of impatient mistrust
Parties separate to the right and left
Which are forms of natural opposites
We tend to accuse each other of theft
Each of us discovers a lens that fits
Each issue involves bolstering details
Everyone gets good at reciting facts
Parties traffic in deception wholesale
Self-righteous believers formulate packs
The cosmos creates the opposing poles
It is only human to play our roles.

Liberty
opposes
equality —
there never is
a lasting
victory.

Cid's Gift

Greg Dunn and I were kicking around in
Kyoto Japan sharing our interest
In poetry — teaching English — and *Zen* —
And both of us were on a wordy quest
For enlightenment expending our youth
In exotic surroundings while married
To *Japanese* women and seeking truth
As expatriates living in a blend
Of cultures when Greg suggested that we
Reach out to a famous poet who lived
In *Kyoto* — *Cid Corman* — we schemed to see
Whether he would workshop with us to feed
Our heads — and he was a beatnik guru
And we hungered for verbal jujitsu.

Cid lurched from a bus
wearing a beret holding
a briefcase with a
face projecting authority
and cranky intelligence.

One isn't sure where one is traipsing to
Until an actual arrival and
In the bloom of youth it's easy to
Imagine the future beckons with fecund
Fortune and I was saturated with
Bookish ambition but hadn't yet met
A genuine poet boasting a pith
Of accomplishment and casting a net
Of ascendancy about himself so
When we met I *babbled* about writing
My sonnets believing that that would go
Far to *boggle* him without my knowing
In his opinion sonnets were *piffle*
And what I'd written so far was *drivel*.

Cid wasn't crudely
brutally belittling
but he did deftly
expose the panorama
of my simple ignorance.

Every other Sunday afternoon we
Met in my little living room sitting
Like the *Japanese* on the *tatami*
And the three of us would be blathering
For several hours and I mustered my
Courage and read my poems and Cid let
Greg criticize first which electrified
Me because Greg's pronouncements became threats
To my ego and then Cid would have a
Go and would challenge every choice of word
Or he would question an angle of the
Composition — I could be assured
Something would be brought to my attention
Which would befuddle my comprehension.

I'd be upended
yet again deflated by my
surprising foibles
which only strengthened my
determination to write.

Cid provided us with the conceit that
We were undergoing a discipline
And Cid really was a cat with éclat
And I kept schlepping my poetry in
While he repeatedly dangled me by
A foot or batted me about with a
Paw and I worked to clarify my eye
But there were too many words within a
Ten-syllable line and the grammar was
Tricky and rhyming was out of fashion
So I quit composing sonnets because
They were hard to defend depending on
My inexperience and innocence
Compounded by my naïve diffidence.

I realize now
that any poem can be
criticized to death
by any sourpuss so
workshops are only a game.

Sitting at the feet of the guru is
A worthy game and it's helpful to be
Sincere and single-minded and Cid was
Playing the role of trickster splendidly
Dangling his approval just beyond our
Reach which impelled me to scour my mind for
Something solid to stand against his sour
Critique and I contrived so much to pour
Moxie into clever words but looking
Back it's clear I hadn't digested my
Life enough so that I began writing
Poetry into stubby lines that tried
Too hard neglecting superfluity
Unconsciously brazen frivolity.

It takes just enough
experience and patience
to dangle amid
emptiness until the words
appear and fall into place.

The group grew beyond the three of us when
We advertised in *Nara* and *Kobe*
And *Osaka* and we became a den
Of gypsies coming for a colloquy
Of blatherskite — *and the portion of talk*
Devoted to critique wasn't so much —
Cid brought his correspondence taking stock
Of the lives of a fellowship of such
Poets that he came to know around the
World and mostly we discussed the hardships
And adjustments people invent in the
Way of life-jarring puzzles that eclipse
Reasonable expectations that do
Push people in extremis to muddle through.

We mostly discussed
epitomes of
humanity and
perplexities of
personalities.

Cid had an ego like an Abrams tank
Armored and lumbering ahead with a
Steely resolve crushing his doubts with swank
Swiveling the cannon of a pooh-bah
But in the tale of his correspondence
His large compassion was apparent in
His gusty battle against despondence
Trading news and courage as a linchpin
Within his writing fellowship and it's
Sad he had no bulwark of surety
To bolster friends — he only had his wits
And honesty and solidarity
To give his friends because life was a *void*
And belief in holy rescue — *devoid*.

Life to Cid was a
celebration of the
assertion of friendship
and love in an otherwise
meaningless existence.

I was an addict with several years
Sobriety which was long enough to
Experience raw resentment and fear
Without the numbing of the drugs we do
To avoid emotions and I knew that
Cid's attitude wasn't what I wanted
To stay healthy and I accepted that
Reliable strength was what I needed
Believing with other addicts like me
It wasn't necessary to define
What the power was or how it helped me
But that I was much better off aligned
With the something-or-other that druggies
And alkies use when they aren't on a spree.

Every addict and
alcoholic who wants to
be sober can find
unsuspected sources of
strength to grow roots into.

My job was to teach English at Berlitz
And I could rejigger my schedule to
Teach double time which allowed me to split
For a week off which I was eager to
Do driving through *Honshu* to a city
Called *Obama* on a bay of the Sea
Of Japan to the temple *Hosshin-ji*
Where for an expanse of five centuries
The *Japanese* practiced *Zen* and upon
My arrival on Sunday night I would
Go to the *zendo* alone to sit on
A *zafu* to meditate and I would
Sink into a warm bath of *samadhi*
Of a vibrating surge of rhapsody.

My first taste of *Zen*
by myself in the empty
zendo clued me
into the fact that I had
opened a profundity.

I started on my trips to the temple
Zooming on a racy motorcycle
But over years I deescalated
Being differently motivated
I sold my snazzy supersonic bike
For a newspaper delivery bike
I took me triple the time to arrive
But my sensibilities came alive
I was hunting in each fleeting second
For that one metamorphizing moment
It could come inside a cedar forest
At a coffee shop when taking a rest
There were swift mountain streams along the way
And I absorbed the ocean on the bay.

I thought something
could happen any
second upon the
winding road amid little
mountains and thatched villages.

A *Zen sesshin* is a week of endurance
Could magic happen? There's no assurance
The object is to give up desires
By desiring not to desire
It becomes an elusive state of mind
As a contradictory double bind
The spine must be tensed and rigidly straight
The strain initially is very great
As the week goes on the energy builds
And one is silently struggling until
A point comes when the sitting is easy
And a superabundance is breezy
Which is the joy of effortless effort
To reach this point one crosses a desert.

Sesshin is also like
hiking a mountain
with straining labor
in the first few days.

After the sticking point comes clarity
There is an electric serenity
The temple bell is cleanly resonant
The sun on the cedar slopes is brilliant
I fall in love with simple rituals
Being fully absorbed in eating meals
Between sittings I sit on a stone step
There seems no end of exuberant pep —
I could never quite dislodge my ego
And I still don't know how to let it go
But I have entered on the Buddha way
Believing freedom could happen today
My practice is a daily flirtation
Of trudging the road to liberation.

The *Zen* master raised and struck
a staff on the *tatami*
saying "with wholehearted
effort you cannot
miss."

Cid did have international readers
Who were a network of well-read writers
Every session of our group he brought stuff
To read which was plenty reason enough
To keep our group curiously engaged
The cynosure of Cid's life was arranged
Around the skillful expression of words
The predicament of each is absurd
Isolated solace needs to be shared
He loved the skillful leverage that bared
The offbeat cusp of snow of touch of mood
The delicacy of hearts pumping blood
He had an eye for quirky bravery
Clever pugnacity was savory.

By listening to
the stuff that Cid brought to read
one gained a taste of
what *worked* in the writing — the
words had a *hearty* impact.

Cid was impervious to Buddhahood
He disbelieved traditional sainthood
He admired offbeat characters with nerve
Who resisted the void of death with verve
He probed the *meaning* of meaninglessness
Didn't see *pregnancy* in emptiness
We could only accept him as he was
He knew he'd be forgotten — *and he is* —
I had the gusto of sitting with him
Our sessions were lively — *they were not grim* —
After hours of talk my head was tired
With more nutrition than I could acquire
Yet Cid was a connoisseur of sorrow
I carry his essence in my marrow.

The essence of
the famous passes
imperceivably
into those they
touched.

Harada Sekkei was a *Zen* master
Who was another excellent trickster
He practiced the quizzing art of *koans*
By presenting riddles that felt like cons
Is there really a sensible answer?
One suspected he's a necromancer
He used his staff to strike the *tatami*
Pronouncing that the pursuit is easy
Wholehearted effort brings liberation
Clarity does come — *after frustration* —
Thirty years later I am still seeking
The pith of the *koan* is intriguing
His clear example is hard to dismiss
When aiming for the floor — *how can you miss?*

Before my return to
America in our
last private interview
he filled my abdomen
with a warmth of glowing
love.

Do I have to choose between these two?
I love Cid's knowledge and clever voodoo
His emblazoned words are lovely dancers
For difficulties he had no answers
He didn't address quixotic ego
Of sweet sorrow he couldn't let go
There's the folly of king on the mountain
A game to be played again and again
One wins by being the cleverest cat
When playing the game — *I feel like a gnat* —
For thirty years I gave up poetry —
Putting effort in finding clarity
Beginning each day with meditation
I am dancing with my expectations.

The real trick is
to quietly
sit letting thoughts
freely arise
and dissipate
innocently.

One day a metaphor enchanted me
My mind is bowl — *open and empty* —
Here is jubilation — *playing with words* —
It is propitious to be absurd
Do we have to take life seriously?
I indulge a healthy rascality
For six years I have written sonnets
Once started again I couldn't stop it
I think about Cid — *he helps me to smile* —
His cranky sincerity was worthwhile
I do what I love — *I'm sure he'd agree* —
That my sonnets are cheerful bumblebees
Like any good trickster he had a *plan*
Cid Corman is the *man* — I am a *fan*.

—*Tekkan*

You touch me
and I grow —
you take me

and I am —
we are no
one alone.

—*Cid Corman*

www.ingramcontent.com/pod-product-compliance
Lightning Source LLC
Chambersburg PA
CBHW062040290426
44109CB00026B/2688